ON THE
WAY

WILLIAM BROOKS
AND
DR. GEORGE SAYRE JR.

ON THE
WAY

ARPress
45 Dan Road Suite 5
Canton, MA 02021

Hotline: 1(888) 821-0229
Fax: 1(508) 545-7580

Ordering Information:

Quantity sales. Special discounts are available on quantity purchases by corporations, associations, and others. For details, contact the publisher at the address above.

Printed in the United States of America.

ISBN-13:   Softcover   979-8-89356-204-0
                eBook   979-8-89356-205-7
                Hardback   979-8-89356-206-4

Library of Congress Control Number: 2024905430

Table of Contents

DEDICATION

This wondrous book would NOT be in existence without the support and endurance and kindly affection toward their husbands thus provided by Suzanne Lee Brooks and Jeanine Baker.

George and I are but clumsy roustabouts. The Ladies on the other hand are Most Royal and Elegante'.

Thank you good souled Ladies for all your faith filled help...and patience!

WB+ et GS

 ❧ WILLIAM BROOKS AND DR. GEORGE SAYRE JR.

Prologue to *On the Way, a small book*

THEN THE LORD said, "Leave your own country and your kinsfolk and your
    friends,
And your house; And go to a country that I myself will show you. I will bless
    you that you may become a blessing for others that they too may see."
Inspired by Genesis 12:1-2: "Hear my friend-a breaking
Soundlingful brook streaming. Behold it is the Bonet running through
    Dromahair."

From *On the Way*, db+

On the Way

Feel the fullness of all the feelings

Do not select and sift

Feel them as they are aroused.

Be about the divine business of … being on the way

And as you awaken listen further or closer the soundingnesses

Hear my friend a breaking soundingful brook streaming.

Behold it is the Bonet running through Dromahair.

See past the foggy shadows and dappled gray hear passed the over

cluttered air the silences that are but creeped and blissful and kind

bent by ancient time

Plant the panting heart that darts here to there and back again

Looking for respite and finding none

For rest is in the silences tucked onto water sounds and lights gentled by

holiness and prayer founding its soul

For we are all already on the way

we are all beside one another

We are found in the divine by being at one.

Mullaghmore Head

Mullaghmore Head, king of perspective

On the Atlantic oblique castle set

Near Tullaghan and its sweet effect

Kinlough gales with bird's breath

Sky second ground to mountainview

Prodigious painterly skies do bring

Close the day's engine extravagant

Thus thrilling the sense's elation

Allowing the soul to plant and soar

At once a resplendent introspect.

The Bonet's Rush

It runs along a split rail fence

Over the splintered spine of rocks ancient

A richly enthused rush flows with sturdiness

Steps taken next it are to be care-filled

Since no created path banks its interest

Rather the rush is the jubilant waters

Aged and bearded the water hosts an eternal spirit

Elegant as the arched foot of a ballerina on stage

Seasons of unrelenting magic magnify the glistening surface

Creative fieriness well-calibrated accompanies each stroller

Clad in mortal fabric and substance as they think their thoughts

Far passed mere sinews and bone and flesh adhered

All along Bonet's graceful flow, yet powerful grasp for

The waters roil shaped and swayed by nature's innovation

Are the blank canvas of remembrance and history of love

And friendship back home neatly tucked in to fondness forever

the Bonet speaks many languages as striking as glossolalia

And heals ailments simply by her charm and hastens time

Into a harmonious oneness incarnate

Great trunked trees gnarl upward

like crazed pillars on one side of the run

mixing shadowed strengths with velveted darkness

The feeling of the sorcerer's wish come to substantiate reality

As Patricus's church bell appeals to souls, "Come to Mass."

Fairy Door

Facilitate our imagining powers

To endear ourselves to the hour

Of fascination's dream

All for a tiny door insinuated into a tree

Of all things magnificently inferred

On a forgotten road

From yesteryear so alive today.

Door in a Tree

Singing in the misted froth
The little people are said
To be hereabouts using magic
And to espy all human doings
Our forays into local gossip
And socialized medicine
And work and family chores
And friends on different shores
Sublime are these fairy folk
Looking in on us unaware of their looking
Presence so close yet undetectable are they
Using ancient ways to insist on knowledge
A drenched drizzle murmurs around the tree
Tender ears and achingly strained eyes
Peal for the child's inborn curiosity
and older hands tighten with arthritis
Like artistry to hold a pen or host the child's questioning
"The wonder of it all; can you imagine?"
A small wooden door and frame strike awe in the old heart
Buoys the cords of beating drums inside the skin.
Youth knocks on this door often.
It is accessible and friendly all the while
Being standoffish. Quite the fascinating draw.
Consider the possibilities this door presents
Rather represents...
Extraordinaire: an appeal to the gazer
To live younger inside out.

The Small Tree Door

The journeyed one who travels without a map

nary a hope can endure

The peasant, however, travels light upon the moor

Only what they wear and the little pack-knap.

Yet surprises dawn in the least expected place

Thus to discover

A tiny door for elfin folk to therein hover.

And exist all this time with not a discernible trace

Thus a photographer and his mate a mere poet

Were stubbed to astonishing stop

And roared backward in their drop

Jawed new to espy and with attention to know it.

And thus the photographer

Did it photo

And because of whimsy's art can show

That any can learn to become an iconographer.

"Every Hour" Counts

Inspired by William Butler Yates

"Every hour carries a new challenge"

Under a Celtic sky labored with fantastic clouds

A heavy blanket of moist air hovers over Dromahair

Also an extravagant hush makes elegant the site

Tall grasses now bent and trampled down

By the jackboots worn of rain and snow

The sheer beauty of winter's power is felt

Next hour the skies come

apart and flow in white gray rivers

Elating the artistic senses

Arran, thou art a well-intentioned land

With mild people obliged to welcome

With sky and mountains touching like old friends

Hand to hand each second minute

Is gifted over to the next to weave an hour

And every hour brings with it a new world

The Hybernian Shield

Invested-enfolded

In quatrafoil field

Shining loughs to reflect the revived human spirit

The refreshed, awakened heart atop the dramas

The rejuvenate reasoning so easily accommodated

ratiocinari a relocation of center

A force of life's creative will

A participle of the desire to thrive in hope

To embrace the rugged beauty availed

And breathe at last the golden shimmer

Ireland, you above the rest make welcome true

Sliabh League

High-placed steeps of challenge

Not yet yielding a steady ground

Carved and worn down by winters

And unblown glassy tide

And ram's horn curly variegated hammering

Against solid rock face unyielding but wearing down

Nonetheless two opposites, wind and stone

And the omnipresent waves crashing and smashing and tearing at

The carpeted grasses various crawling the shoreline

Like a wooly caterpillar slow and cumbersome to travel

The waters below surge and tide and evince and grate

These darned waters stained by time dare life itself

With a knowing grin and a leap at the junctions too tall to reach

This is the knife edge of the world

This is the sidestepped steep sculpted as offertory to heaven

Sliabh League is God's foot stool

For Glenn Columcille the resting place of spark and spirit

For Christ's unparalleled face beaming down to tundra soils

Combined with choirs long silenced from ruins once living

Now shuttered and shadowed and haunted

But pointing the way back to freedom and artists' manner.

Lyric Innisfree–Lough Gill

a glade of beesong

a lap of wave

precise not gone wrong

but to hear and bear out soul's crave;

angels all alaughter

along shore's delicate line

heaven's own rafter

to uphold sun's shine

earth slows now

its turn - not fast

noon hosts its own cow

the cool whitte lasts

the milk of refine

the tincture of scale

supply the thirst's parched place

as cool as iced hail.

 WILLIAM BROOKS AND DR. GEORGE SAYRE JR.

The Woody Tree Forest

Cedar wool blankets laid out across acres

Startling timber statuesque predominate

A velvety tower in soldier watch stance

Enthralls, astounds, astonishes the eye;

Even the fairy folk, the little people

Of Hibernian forests catch the bats

And listen to their night-songs and write tunes

In order to celebrate the season next.

Bursting with nature's inordinance

the turns of shadow swallow the landscape

And belch out the hedgerows along the small paths of journey.

Resonate with Celtic applause for entertainment

Even lane and roads are elegantly charming neighbors to call upon

And nature's old self handy at many trades

Plays at being in place uniquely made of dreams

Ether and cloud the only substance to the vision

Quarter-light turns yet again a notch on the wheel of time

Adding a mixture of verdant luxury covering with the

Fully intoxicating mind's eyeglasses with cheered successions.

Wm. Butler Yates wrote,

"Our feet would linger where beauty has lived"

It takes a special heart driven driver-eye

To capture "the moment." On film or in conversement.

Trees, lichen, ancient rock formations, shadow, cliffs and glades

Defend dense fog with a balmy sunshine by afternoon

Sunlight sets the scars in motion to travel the skies by indigo night.

Lighting the patterns of days gone by and whose ways have

Crossed over into the forgotten manner and lexicography of wisdom.

once held so much of the world's sway and assessment, wisdom

The keeper of the Temples now is not fond of the labor required

To embolden the spirit's release and formation into feathered wing.

Thought err times zones and counties proper

The driver drives his machine into spring and then summer

And summer into Indian spring and autumn and then winter, which catches all

by the throat and squeezes hard the air passage almost closed off.

Be gone, you unruly seasons, be more rested next time you drop by and more

cheery too. So Jaun Jorge studied the practice of teething and dental

stress even in dismal summer albeit Hawyi as reward for war fought.

Even then his virtuosity was known far and wide and coast to coast.

Humble yet strong, delightful yet impish...

a finesseir of souls and one-sided banter

To set aright the broken bridge or the tortured bicuspid.

To set to rights all monthly wrongs of occasion and happenstance.

Here and there spiced by elegant humor ever at a chance to shine

Worthy is this crafter of doors and trunks and gates and desks and chairs.

And once upon a time dentured selves

the carpenter's hands guide Jaun's hands,

hands of a similar carpenter on the north ledge of the Galilee whose traded

gold-weighted words and images and metaphors and quips stand

 time; these are the Sophia logia chat tickle Jorge's fancy and

vocabulary

Thus in the gracious light of generosity's engine

Unpayable is the debt I owe him for ferrying the likes of moi

All over Erie-land of Hibernian-psyche and domain of wonder.

Thank you, Jaun Jorge, for the spirit of a saint that holds thee fast.

Five thousand years back, the La Grange Mound stirs attention and

obeisance still felt and rediscovered on a daily basis. A beehive inside

a mountain how wonderfully exquisite and upside down like the Celts themselves.

Jorge Von Juan d' Universe is the embodiment of a friend and a fellow

sojourner, a kind of sacred elfin one caught by circumstance and held

in place to teach and persuade and define and make material for

physical beings who themselves are just discovering the journey is

shorter than announced and longer than strength is able to hold.

But Jaun Jorge holds and holds on for life dear...as driving force to

discover grace in every next setting, be it geographic metaphysical or

ivory-silvered-earthen.

Bee-Song-Yes

Diminishment is not a cradle song

unchecked greed not a motto to uptake

Redirection of truth is not justice secured

But blackened shoot on the soul pure plain.

Sorrow entrenched sets teeth on edge

Lost hours become years evidenced

Wonder only the unwearied wing

Above the fray and planted chaos

Charmed allure is the transfiguring bell

Tinkling out melodious over ancestral mounds

Lightning hurling triumphs across itself

In honor of heaven's throne radiant

Memory binds a tether to thriving

As bee-musics drench the cold air

Honey is being made but unseen at this vantage

Nevertheless its sweetness shall be tasted

In the eventual dawning of the present moment

Awarding all, the precursor of celebration arriving.

A library's worth of mad exaltations

The extant insects make sweetness real

Valued for its golden glow as well as refine

For the grace to be shared out among

The masses gathered for sustenance.

So grace and joy may be known and sampled

Consumed for fire to exile pain's former thunder

"Comfort ye" once did sing the song

And now is as good as any to be recomfort'ed

Rest the frenzied moan et sigh

Take breath to inhale holiness, exhale

Inhale, granting the oxygenation of forgiveness

Most like forgiveness long overdue

Take the mill wheel a turn toward Qodesh

Repatriate humor's storehouse with Auguste. Yes

Yes...beesong singing...

Gifted Mages Two Before

Confidence anew, again the young poets excel

In being dependent, scared, ardent too

Corseting requirements only to obey to dedicate all

to the Logos Incarnate, impecunious of focus

Restless worriers of innocent worry fear and childlike dread

Collecting sprites and fairies,

Red and white vintage bottled spirits each

No wine bag for these collectors, only the freshest bottle

Glimmering with ornate sparkle and charm as "acceptable"

Scored quickly, leafy branches anticipate their due

And respond to the encouraging words offered on the floor of the vineyard

Looking up the poets would recite their-leaden-best to encourage the vines to

Produce and yield; multiply and delight the eye with verdancy, unrivaled

The taste buds with confounding bittersweet complexity.

The seed of contentment barely known to this day

Had been sown in the original garden of harmonies combined

Of Adam et Aeva gifted mages for the nomenclating of things

Now gifted mages today walk overconfident of their prowess

Yet diffident chill winds unsettle these untested ones so young

Confidence is in hope not in skill nor scepter, the ancient poets remind:

No blade of the realm in-orbed by reign shall protect

Ultimately, rather the unvarnished word, honestly utter'd in humiliatas of the

highest value,

These are the coins of the king that effect spending

Not the pretty shiny things, bribed out "on the take" atmosphere

but the honest sincerities offered fully

at supreme cost

Vocabulary vaunted vestments display a manner of eloquence with

designer labels hanging down with $ price

But the quiet unassuming ancients

these poets kept to the close

To the cathedral's round wall and shadows

for here—in these divine prescinds

therein urgent fertile deep shadows enthrall, the true-song.

Angels need no bottles nor scripts nor music writ

not even instruments of acumen nor skill

For they are already in the presence of the Vintner of all sound and beauty

of taste and eloquence and art

Which no earthen vessel may contain but only anticipate.

seek rather the things invisible,

if wealth it is

ye seek.

Henry David Thoreau once observed beware of any endeavor that

requires a new pair of shoes ut-oh

Sometimes officiants at weddings get carried away with the sentiment or the

wondrous sounding of too many words

So not wanting to speak over-much and long-some-ly

I will share something this inspired by/for you two

becoming one in God's higher math called marriage divine and

harmonious Seeing, breathing, taking in-and spinning in one's mind

The excitement and the gathered ones' dear energy of collective well-wishing

We watch as you hold hands and bridge the coming years

By in this moment exchanging vows

making promises built on hope's confident faithfulness...

Creating, transforming second to second to millennia

Now is the fullest of time's moments

yet to be until the next NOW commences

So tread lightly and fly strong as the wind

Mark the canvas of today and write the word of life boldly

Share the call and heed the invitation to adore and absolve and reinvent

always forgive—and be mercy itself

be humble in reception of this sacred gift that heavens throne grants you

send the gift and explode the mystery with embrace and laughter and prayer

Present future—dawning in a diminutive silence, lee it settle

and reassure

Then, verbalizing the exquisite

Now with poetry's yes

Don't forget

But remember, be fond of your togetherness

Re-associate, reintroduce, regain as if for the first time

One another time and again...day in day out

Dig down and surround each other with deep affection

In this holy now live fully

Now is the time

Now is incarnation

now is the moment of beginning +

and it will last forever as God's benediction will bless you always.

Blessed be you as one but as well as uniquely-one another.

Lovingly so...

Columcille Brave

do not forget to save

the next hour to save a chronicled prayer

and to hold it in tone for an hour's care

of such texts as handily writ

and keep thy priestly kit

well-oiled so supple it may be

of use for others to hear and see

for in the night's deep lamp

monkish souls feel the sacred stamp

of God's holy will et wheel

upon the hearts incased in beehive's steel

chanting the moments as whole of praise

and fill the mind's conscious days

with divine and godly ways

unending...

Sw   hop
The
Sweater

Becomingly So+

my ancestors enjoyed none

of the gentle valleys

nor the counties without number

T'was they that found rock's ton

unfathomable to call a ballie

and build a thatch cottage without slumber

Such as Columcille did lumber

and press and dent and stack as sally

making houses of light in which to chant encounter

Ages later now, and time to come

the voices join in office-seal

before Eucharist's meal

becomes...

It's time the light offers a calling sent

forget the hills' invoices and the rent

Pray only homage and art and mysteries

Lord

as if eternal life we can afford

becoming

forever ourselves

and find the sum of creation

that all may learn to be woken

and live the Logos SPOKEN.

BECOMINGINGLY so...

The Angel in the Blue Car

Look left, look right! Adventure

there is a lorrie, and a tiny break in space

Go take it! Go forth and prosper.

we thought there was time enough but time is no human's possession; time is

its own winged thing creaturely

obedient only to the throne of heaven's calling

The nation's highway was less generous than anticipated

unrelenting in its mass and volume and constancy of flow

yet into Corybantic trafficked weeds we went

we flew and almost chewed metal savings and glass yet by some mystic

moment stalled by hands divine

the angel in the blue car sounded and laughing greeting well

timed and a sacred wave or blessing to ensure awakening

rather than obliterate our mortal canister

she with genteel mercy forgave and waved again

as if the first was precursor to the second being the best

benediction of the year or decade, because we lived...

the point is thus, to be sure we were highly preserved from certain demise

and surrender of the life force once taken for granted

Thanks be

Thanks BE to the highest heavens

for the angel in the blue car

gladdened by luster and unearthly kindness awarded.

In Dromahair

Each fire burns differently from the last

Although we build carefully the past

We layer and stack and set

We sweat and refine to get

The flames we imagine as best

In Dromahair we remember the days gone bye

We watch the blaze and wonder and we sigh

We warm hurting hands from the day at sea

We hold the cat stroking his paw upon our knee

These flames we imagine are the certainly best

In Dromahair we gaze into the deeps of the fire

We settle in to contemplate the history of our ire

We hum to drive away the pain's domain with glee

We gently mouth the silent words that set us free

This foe is truly a friend found

In Dromahair

I sing not as often as I had

Yet I long more than ever for the sad

The ones who have no fire, no car, nor roof

The ones who think all others remain from them aloof

This fire is a startling blaze

In Dromahair we close not the lid

Of celebration's glory that were never hid

But lived largely from the heart

And included the shewing sound of art

This fire warms the soul of a new start.

The Wing et Candle's Heat

At evening's dusking

Just as the light dims inside the room

The temperature lessens with a sigh

Observed et observer unite in creation

Fire that fascinates can also harm

A double charmed effect

Complex beauty intensifies the wing

Of a shiny moth on the prowl

Beauty et vision

Proximity et juxtaposition

Close-near, far enough then again

Moth et flame's bud

Reaching up like a finger pointing

Dark then light refracted and opposed

Dance step and jig and turn and stop

Best be going, little insect, this is a dangerous joust

one not intended for the inattentive

Before anything amiss strikes out

Be off into the dust-moted air

Little one

Before tragedy strikes

And smolders the dream active

Best be launched into that cool thinness

Sunset soft illumined by golden pink

Dazzling yet calming all at one

This candle can do but its employ

That is to burn brightly as a torch beam

To illumine the truth as art's reality itself.

Coldness itself dresses the stone

Baptizes the bone of soul

Chill completes the midnight bed to wooden cross

An altar book as top stone rests-open, inviting...

Rattled reddened blistered hands turn pages

Christ before

Christ to come

Christ in the here and drenched bleak NOW

Consider the merit of standing inside this temple

A mansion and cave, a barn and a receptacle

A place for singing salvation into daystar light

Constructed in the ancient manner

Stone upon slant upon stone, a knowledge lost

Forgiveness still labors in this Chantry Especial

Calling to all humankind to rejoice and be glad

Resonate soundings reverberate, vibrate, stir

Bouncing off hard shell starts and fits of voceration

Lined with intercession and fervent hopes unending

Not wielding here, nothing but faithfulness supreme and unmasked

Hard-won and gentle-natured reviving day to night to morning

The flat stone floor moves with the cant, rocking as a saw

The vibration and timbre of voice thrills the air

Underfoot percussive rhythm supports yet suggests

That the singer at his song-filled praise might be care-filled for balance.

A "sensing angel" delivers a new bounty of illumine in logia

To add to the small candled tapers shining with all their will

Through a tiny window comes the morning brightness

Cheering the graystone light into a golden hued delight

Brightness upturned to conical and canyon liturgy

Now filed as offered in Sienna and umber, but never complete,

Merely offered, as life and gentle smile. Upon fate's feet standing…

The Office in Beehive

Small corralled cone

Spiritual upturned grace reigning downing yet heavenwardly

Side stepped no longer but full throated and flat dance shoe well planted

The tones cold churned into delicate ice sculptures

Chant and vox not one, not too much

But just as would be thought appropriate for the setting

Nicely done this office coming from the soul's basement

Warmed spirit takes away the chill fathomless mystery

And turns Easter back to earthen gift as well spring for thirst

The small west window brooks a life form of yellow ocher

The venting of breath Ale'd last night but dried by this morning rise

God the Mystery nothing lacking, nothing wanting, nothing needed

Is at one in harmonic unity of accord

Now the symphony of quiet may wash the innards of the cavity

Roughhewn but pleasant and plain as holiness

Priestsong lingers in this place springing with animation

Known by heart as logia magnum

Or bonum majestica explica

The voices of past trill in present future

Tremulating the chill again as if to awaken the senses

The world is healed once more by a sealed cloth book

and office lived as breath upon the Atlantic belief

crossing the channel to serve the day born soon.

Oratorio

Oratorio, my dwelling sanctuary

Library of hallowed thought

Enchiridion

The home of instruction extraordinaire

Cave of knowledge fortifying elixir

The savor of healing ointment revives

Lair of lingering anointing

Correspondent winged seraphim

Carpeted allegory

Dropped in harmonics resplendent

Vented by desert breezes

Enlightened, illumined by experience

Oratorio lift my senses high breath in me

Let me be strengthened built and made proficient

Creative resolute in darkness and aimed toward light.

My Soul Doth Magnify the Lord

My inner-most spirit

Hath highly and heartily made magnification

An excited extraordinaire exclamation to Thee O Lord

For you are ever with me, us with the Oneness of all Things Made

You only have made us and not we ourselves

Although we oft image we are wily and imaginative as you at times

Those days we feel cocky and arrogantly superior

For some these are most days; for your other saints

It's only about a day and half each week. I am one of these

So in the mystery of unity and harmonics

You attract us to being at one with the creation and creatures

We often look at fellow creatures forgetting who made them

and for the purposes of holiness and inspiration they divinely serve, not

for own dominion nor our procession

We own nothing

and only decide "our own" thinking

At best yet when we think we have

Or should have control we blunder as toddlers off balance

Rather I rejoice in my poverty of humanness

Not wanting anything simply because of its sheer beauty and originality

Outpace my ability to properly appreciate what all is gifted moment to

moment

Gratitude is the best companion. Amen.

Isle Chantry

Darkness and light interweave as hands at prayer

Forming a domicile of cone shape in winter's sleet

A prayerful light transforms those inside this place

Incense and psalms wonder around like children at play

Offertory sacrifice of

Passionate contemplation arises as the candle smoke

Hitting the frozen air and the deepest indigo hue of faith at work

As others sleep

Thanksgiving and exhalations round the stone walls in

circles unending Inspiring the chanter to continue the chorded thought

Trinitarian indeling sparks Magnificat thrice

Reminding of bygone years and dreams strewn forward

this is worship unseen by most and unknown by more

This is the cavernous gratitude in ascendency

Stone upon Prayer builds character

Tides of music flow in and out with the oceanic sway

Faith's drumming counts the moments next born

Association grown fond warms the convivial sound

Produced to be a joy and a hope finding

Alliances are made with the earth and air and rock

now these are the chorus

These the angels in pursuit of delight celestial.

A Pointing Feather Found

A pointing feather found

Monks incorporate pointing feathers

to precede the pointed notes of music

Chanted from books for the divine offices

Pointing feathers are blest and most prized

It has been said seven wells make an ocean

But it only takes one well to be marked as "holy"

One holy well is enough for an entire nation

much less one in every county...

Many thousands of waves show an ocean as "sea"

But only one well can offer oceanic hope for the "dismayed"

Faith and hope and love can dwell in a drop of water "blessed"

And one drop of water can quench the hottest soul "tormented"

Hundreds of birds allow an

Exhalation of sheer breathing exaltation

One monastic can chant hundreds of logia

but one need be hallowed to enthrall

And only one pointing feathered discovered on lonely Innesmurray

Is enough to have made the entire 34 days' journey "a wonder"

Sometimes even one alone

is more than enough

to please and thrill and enchant

a chanter of song.

No One Dare

No one dare

No one dare risk so much

This human journey so precious and wrought with danger

But what of the fates and

The shadow of the divine?

A kind of lack becomes acceptable coinage

A spreading contagion free to express

Without measure one's full discontent

We ache for the beauteous in logos, for joy

In the flesh, incarnate by color-shape-texture

In the eyes of the familiar stranger, a nod.

In the hand of trust extended from a wheeled chair

A hospital gurney or proximate to a just closed door

Or in the child upon the circle rug gathering patience

Yearning to keep secret that we do not hold

To embrace those we do not know

To garner strength that is not inherently our own

As once toward Emmaus

Walk as companion now good friend

Walk within as well as alongside

Make us to soar in our treading

Perhaps as if flying in common place

Open the mystery of hearing intelligence

By saying:

"Harmony can be touched"

By becoming the walk itself

singing the journey song expressed

Incarnation is host yet again

Enigmatical wonder invitatory: wonder extolled.

Donegal

Donegal arrogant in size alone

Daunting presence

First in size, dominate in atmosphere

Porcelain of sudden adventures

Sitting atop the over grand mountain

Dramas all and each like camels on the run

How did You come to nature so fully?

And how have you nurtured both snow and ice, sun and wind

All at once?

It seems You have come to know silence as strength

A roughhewn figure cut by time, etched by eons

Manner is how you saunter through the seasons

Yet timeless and well placed.

Donegal's Tory

Tory North to North East's Pointing

Ontology well past knowing

Here black moths turn toward dawn

Blue to sun's setting will have to wait

With peneplain rocks casting spells

Magic potions of mists rising effortlessly

Waves and sea salt savor the shoreline

Dividing the water from the sky and sea from dry land

Puffin's breath and sardined brine meal invite hunger

Carpenter birds build and feast upon worms and ants

Winds worth of strength push aside noon day

And even-song winds its way toward the shore

Toraighed presence making for a fixed repeal

of horizon's faults lines, fixed and forgiven

Magic bogs and feather grass reach forth

Turfed society and turtle shells line the beach

Passage on the sand leaves no trace of pilgrimage

Lichen pretends to be a baby's age when in fact it is ancient

Earthen forms render subtle the men walking like trees

Unrecompensed fondness for granite seeps upward

So this island is forged in memory with jagged cliffs tall

Salutary and triaged splendor

Sublime supplicants of arched rock kneel at the sun's last gasp

Salted sunlight softens into blanketed mists with brine surprise.

Rock of Ages

Forged in the bowels of Gaia,

Forced out of the furnace depths

To cool on the surface

A rock is born.

Stressed and cracked by the forces of tectonics

Cracked and eroded by geologic principles

Time and nature preparing the outer surface

Rendering it suitable to be placed by a mason

Into the matrix of a wall.

Freestanding, the wall faces the ravages

Of time and nature.

Eventually broken, the wall liberates the rock.

Free from the wall the rock again is washed by time

Until it is again utilized by a future mason in the

Construction of yet another wall.

George Stone Sayre Jr.

West Port

Heading to West Port insect wings hum mercilessly

Releasing the power of fear served sweating

Even though the air outside is iced

Glistening whites of a thousand hued snows gathered

Dialogues open the tomb's door wide and slow

Come out shouts the life voice

Come out and play and inhabit your skin and refresh your mind

Name yourself "ALIVE" and see the difference begin

Air warm and birds thaw out to fly in great giant exaltation

No more ice-picked store angers manicured by incarceration

Strips and stripes of peace break into banners and flags

Kites and songfests breaking forth

No judgment today—ally in free!

Now the insect wings and legs sing chirping much that fills the air

with simple delight

No fear lingers—no cold

No boundless mind-numbing ices struggling

Only frolic as if spring were no longer an idea.

Compestral Leah

CrowRaven fields circumventing hedgerows and lane

Clonmacnoise upon horizon

history's library tower beaming upward toward low clouds

Gray gravy like air covers Temples Conner and Doolin

O'Roukes transport with Curian' spires scratch at heaven's door

The Lough is pure silver and reflective as a mirror

Stoned walls crane with slant and mossed mortar

Civilitas lends the fields a character of yield and promise

Constant stonework is required in this place

Back muscles will ache again and again

Hands rubbed raw to blessing because of stone cuts and harsh wind

Necessitated labor is the daily bread of these who pray and sing mutely

Repair and resolve are ONE.

Collects canted mend fences and despoil hardness

Restocking of hay for roofs top and cattle amuse the gatlings in pasture

Government is inward in the monastic trade. Significant freedom begins

unseen undetected joys ticked the fancy of the workers

Embankments are wild and doors are strong

The will is known as voluntas-is to be tamed

Transfiguring grace comes in a bowl of potato soup and brown bread hard as rock

and looks as if one too

Inevitability schedules its liturgies with intent

And as day comes to a close by light diminishing

The night births itself by song and aligning symmetry of psalter.

Glenn Columcille

Between two dramas, two bald-worn mountains run a valley

Verdant and turfed and thick

A heavy haze pushes down everything in its path and is subservient to none.

Northland is unique with St Peter's Lough over to Ballyswan

The decent into the valley stays the mind and excites the stomach

No words but Irish fill the air

And the sheep

The sheep are in the thousands

Huge piled masses of wool and dirt

Painted faces and trembling singers they are

Running to and fro and upon arrive at the parish church

Named for its saint they run toward the visitor bleating

An unknown chant excitedly sharing a historic take

The song thrills the heart and tickles the ear

The ancient atmosphere and utter softness of atmosphere

Sways the soul itself and soothes the senses.

Durrow Crossing

Fairy roads open the scape

travel your direction as best you

the lanes meander with glee and glenn

Hedgerows creep over the road with abandon

Intensity of Western culture gives way to old ways

And a feel of long ago sprouts like sunflowers

Roads diminishes into lanes and lanes adjust into rutted pathways

Dirt embankments rise as if some ancient animal will appear

shortly to devour all, including the land and byways

A dream come true emerges as Durrow thickens upon the midline

Now to touch the HIGH Cross made by Columcille's hand in artistry

Is all the imagination can bear. Look up and beauty is magnified in light.

Durrow and Columcille as united and melded into the present tense; yes

No words can define nor signify meaning. It is enough to breathe in the presence.

Firesong

I think we have met, you and I

Perhaps not in face recognizable nor place delineated

Perhaps not eye to eye, yet...

We seem to share the same prayer for warmth and heat

In winter's mean shambles of ice upon ice

We share a folded prayer of wood staked just thus and kindled to perfection

For the flue to be operable and open

The flood of smoke arises perfectly upward without a hint of inordinacy

There seems to be one heart beating for this fire

Drumming out a singular beat and rhythm

The wood popping and chirping and exploding in sparks and fits

The grate full to brim with yesterday's load

Shaming me for lack of tidiness

The family of origin would lecture on cleanliness

Brochet, sister, mother, father loved the hearth as do I still and sweet fire

I know we have met before

Your character is too well-defined to allow mistake

You once warmed me many years ago

T remember and recall and am appreciative to the core

You made memory of a saddened evening now smiled upon

No longer tho' but one

we encounter the future met again

Sacred is remembrance that warms.

The Cliff

Parapateo often focused on in-adroitness

The flopping left leg accompanied by a sour foot

One can miss the parts major

Or hidden by glint in the eye

Like living in a dreamscape

Demons and dragons on fire

Chasing fair damsels uphill

And cats down to the well

Before they slip away behind the fence

Winds blow through here like tornadic devices

Convivial gatherings are not a commonality here

Not during winter at least

But spring will come and summer bloom

and autumn advances its pace and subjects

For the moment stunning observation is enough

Conversing with the silence is the banquet

Illuminating eyes reveal all the vocabulary needed

This tall start wall is a curtain or solid iron

Dented and maimed

Reforged and forgotten; rediscovered and lost again

Cold brutal wave—waters slice at the sheet of rock

and gulls glide on updrafts

There are no owners here

Only observers on holiday

to see what the Grand Artist formerly forged for insight.

Creelevea Abbey in the Snow

They of wander want set out for Eric

First through air et cloud et ice

Minus 37 degrees by science

Wind their friend in that it pushed us forward

Rapid as an age wish

But bitter as a frigid look

Wheels aided us to travel with briskness

On a sure foundation of ease

And so from Shannon to Dromahair

To cottage to fireplace

We were able to nestle down into routine

And exploration until we found Creelevea Abbey within

earshot of the cottage

A thrown stone could hit from our Bonet riverbank backyard

The Bonet

The Bonet sings and plays to us each day morning through the dark night

The water runs as the land urges

Up the considered hill of respect

Creelevea stands ancient and dramatic

Quiet and stationary

Standing as it chants past to future forward

Present tense in past participle world

Inaudible psalms and collects admire their own content

Interceding for inhabitants for Dromahair outward to Sligo and the world Passionate
Lenten snow loans testament to the storied past

Content now to stand as grace bestowed

Carrying hundreds of stories silently

Setting them in bejeweled wonder for discovery

Open doors invite inward thought

Appetites worn and wounded both dwell side by side

Co-mingling authoritative doubt and faith's joy

Woven into one tapestry

Exorbitant with calm and suggestion.

Killybegs Boat Rail

The boat rail hosted nine buoys

And a default of ropes intertwined

a mix as rich as an international gathering for linguistics

The cold only added flavor to the impending journey

A rounding at sea to Innesmurray Isle,

abandoned only by humanity

By peopled now with histories imagined

The display of buoys and rope urged an

Exquisite emotional quality quite unforeseen

The knots an art form in themselves and skilled

With intricate charming allure of shadow

Who tied all these knots?

They are perfectly full and functional

They are not unnecessary I am told

Musical in their artistry remembered

No lamentation whatsoever sheepshank, half hitch and Boline

as highly suggested by gulling birds upon wing over head

Beautiful woven dreams these ropes so intentional

As skill birthed them each for purpose and labor specific

Each knot is inhabited by some spirit

And speaks a language all its own

And a distinct air hovers over this boar moored to a wharf

As old as iron

Excellent sea salt bites at the face and roughens the teeth

Mists infused by periodic sunbursts enchant some lanterns

Small light boxes attached to the roof of the cabin for the driver

And captain

Both reddened with time and weather, bent with time

Graceful doings have known this boat for fishing

This time capsule of travel and storm cashing

Wave running and dodging fear's seawall of terror

The Celtic knots on the rope teach and invite

"Monere et delectary" they declare

No enemies have we on this tug

Artistry is all the want we have

History unfolds as the engines start and throb the water underneath.

The journey to Innesmurray takes shape.

Passerine

Non superficial twerking, wagstail awaits

Black feathers tussled all about

To and fro with frenzy frothing

Just for show no doubt

With orange beaks protruding and chests of organs pushed out

The euro robins arrive for spring feeding

in the melting snow of Hibernia Northland

The sun just on the slant upward

Peaking and turning and scratching and bobbing

The dance begins in earnest tapping devouring tasting

Tearing at the frozen cod once fried to piping hot but now cold in the snow

Benumbed but not rigid the birds dance for life

Against the backdrop of starvation if they eat not their fill

They muse labor to enjoy the life of birddog

In flies a tiny specimen

No bigger than a thought

A specimen unbeknownst to the observer

Stripes and variations grays upon blue dots

A stunning beak for one so small

proud brave diminutive

Smaller than the rushes

This mighty little one twerks up a storm

Clearing a path to new banquets

The bold bread and potato await devouring

The little plows his ground

Secure upon his matchstick legs

sturdier than steel this winged wonder

This wagtail poet of feeding shows no signs of stopping

This is a creature on a mission blossoming for breakfast bountiful.

Batbox on Alder

On a loney spindly tree

An alder to be precise

all the way to bare

There is a small attached box

Secured in some magical fashion undetected

The box hosts

Tightly mind you a bat

Some boxes host more

This one just one

Bat

It is winter in Dromahair

The sunlight is weak

It is sparing for only hours

If at all, and no hearth

Inside

There are no windows nor glare

just dark wood

Winter warm up inside the

Batbox

Away out of the wind

The tree is tall so the houseboat sway in the breeze

It must be tender company inside

No staircase for dramatic entrance

Just flatten one's wings and

Crawl upward.

Hold on with bat talon hooks

No rustle one's eyelashes

No room inside this

Small sanctuary

Wings pinned won

No coals by which to warm

One's feet and claws

But whose eyes shine

No matter

The lack of illumine

Inside the batbox resides one given over

to luck

Gifted an humble throne

From which to perch

No shoutouts "ineffable"

nor any scripted praise ensue

A merely sole batfowl

Herein dwells currently

Are there bat-songs

to sing in wintertime night?

Perhaps spring will bring the bat words

To the fore

For singing eloquent content.

A "Massed" Phantasy

Ecclesial bells toll, roll, and charm

Declaiming a mass has commenced for the devout

Anxiety plied high for a few, eager sincerity anticipates

Carried deep within each form of person

All have secrets and fears and hope

All wonder is this worth the effort and pain?

Worship is personal and some like it cold and some wish it hot and bothered

and boiling with hades, shades, and stories

Some like to delight in the content of theological mystery and some the signs and symbols of decades making

As the threshold is crossed so is the head chest and shoulder

Agitation at the reader for mispronouncing place names of the holy land

Ordinary time is left behind and Kyros is entered into

The unmeasurable opus dei

Compendium vade mecum

Primer for observance solemn

Alacrity's best dressed manners on display

Expeditious to full affect

Effect is left to the theologian's plight

And jest from year to year

Examined at least by the doctors of the church

So now the story read

The homily delivered sins forgiven

The absolution derived from grace alone (sola gratia)

The viaticum is consumed and appreciated adored and adapted

Unexpurgated faultlessness reigns for a miller second or two and then creeps in

  lust or hunger or pride

It was wonderful while it lasted

Now the knees may be disencumbered and unweighted

Allowing the creaks and cracks to form according to custom

Befitting a felicitous greeting to one and all as the saints do

Genuflection upon reflection invites harmony and peace as the feet roam

Toward the open chancery door

once more sunlight strikes the face and lips and Sunday is NOW

Accomplished as free and open and ready to be charmed and won

Optimal ambulation allows...restrictions are catered and chained

Now a delectable lunch may enthrall and offer...piggery.

When Saints Chop Wood

November last a saint took up ax

To ancient elm and aldered oaken wood did go

He sweat and spewed and bit and chewed

And made all sounds aimed at the state toward relax

The human machine is intricate

It works the hours round

And in his heart the throb eschewed

His mind's lesser thought—non sophisticate

Hi hands do swell and blister

The skin once rough delays

The necessary bloodied cracks that glitter

The blood of hymns aspiring to saint's whisper

So saints do more than open quiet books

Or merely chant away the day

They calm and teach and instruct and charm

and provide the warmth against the winter of the soul

Today is all one might be promised

"For the world is too much with us"

Tomorrow is just anticipated dream quest

But now is the holy moment living; the presence and the gift.

Esah

The force of beauty nomenclated as Esah

Divine Providence furthered

Provocative and enthralling

No punishment Esah

Only golden forgiveness and refreshing wonder

Release of blessings

Enrichment of the poor spirit

The deepest calling yet

Uncorrupt invisible content

Consecrated enthusiasm

Uncalculating charm

Enthused reasoning

Generosity's pledge.

Serious Work

How these eternal

omnipresent

Milk cows cavort

With countless sheep bleating

On verdant stoned walled carpets of grass

In pastures soft with manure

And close cropped by sheep previously

for after biting is disallowed

while chiming the chew

All incessant work

for four stomached ones

Laborers of the field like St Francis's friars

Culling wheat for bread

Rain or sun

Nothing stops the chew

For the milk must be made blessed

poured consumed and nothing

Can stop the chew

Serious work

to be accomplished

in a mere lifetime.

Lough Gartan

Bedrock it is called by most

Not for its genteel softness but rather kept

For an 11 "sleeping stone" by Columcille at Glennveagh.

Glennveagh is a hard place to be sure.

Some say it is the birth place of Columcille.

The place hosts white difficultly barren white stone.

It is here most say that the saint's mother, herself a sainted soul bled white blood during Columcille's birthing. The smallish saint is always depicted as wearing white with white hair. A white horse had Columcille. The man-ghost like winter bleached milk. He is frozen to the place of Glennveagh by love's adoration. Lough Gartan is close enough to see the place lavish in comprehensive beauty but remarked by white flagstone crafted out of loneliness and the bedrock of faith so strong it is ageless.

Like Jabcob at the Jabbac Fiord so Columcille is anchored by his birthing place so near Lough Gartan and Glennveagh.

Count

How long since you have suffered great beauty?

The ache of God's artistry in observing sheer marvel

Full unresting balance, natural exaltation of form

Unbridle your fettered feet for freedom's jaunt

Crack open the timid "yes" to rejoice in music's unfurling

Stretch forth the once forlorn knee or hip

Pour forth the wanderlust that leads to discovery

Bury the choking grief that held your heart in chains

Awaken consciousness

Dare to be overwhelmed by lingering triumph,

Charging imagery...

Arch of Stars

Rich and subtly

A wealth in time

Avast intricate cast of hills nearby

L'A Contemplatio say the mystics

Directed toward advance meditation D' plurals is time 3

Hagios communities processing toward the table facing eastward

An arch of stars overhead pointing to eternity and bliss

We have cosmic allies reads the script

Generations have gathered here and chose gone by still present.

Do this and live eternally starting now.

On the hill a warrior sits atop a steed

The elements his only cloak

Not dressed in sky but cloaked in elements of history

He is dressed as austere bur unpuritanical

No Dracula he nor commonplace soldier but a leader of souls

Not fearless but committed and devoted to growth and change for the
greater good.

For his worth and value lie deep in heaven and not upon earthen clay

This ensign allows rather than retracts as is usual practice now in various
once grand lands

The fact that hatred and evil are truly alive and thriving

that buying and selling of fellow humans is not history bur modern day
    realities

Many are shot for being alive

many hoard for fear of diminishing return on their investments and few invest
    themselves fully in the neighbor much less the stranger.

DO unto others is a faded memory

He's not heavy, he is my brother, now a lost sacrifice

Where are the Brahyans of ancient Celtic culture?

If one stole bread, he was sentenced to become a baker's novice for seven

years creating a new baker and keeping jails free of hungry teens

grace treats souls as better citizens

no raw power unbridled and grievously fierce.

The sword is for truth not hurt

If one were born out of wedlock in other places in Irish lands

one was made an abbot or bishop or abbess,

where is such wisdom today?

Where is gratia bonum to carry on our mistakes as forgiven?

How shall we navigate the days ahead if we host no praxis without wisdom?

The arch of scars still illumines hearts everywhere. The arch is still strong and

seeking to instruct. But all must apply to enter thereupon such

gracious paths.

If I Give Him to You

If I give you him whom I love

sister sea—shall you return the favor of him to me?

Are we sisters, family still? Or are you greater and I lesser bm you detest the

demarcation?

Are you Queen and I mere handmaiden?

Look into my tear-stained and nightless eyes so swollen

Look into my heart torn as by hurricane and fierce wind

Look at my body torn and wracked by grief,

Can you not fully detect my plight and estate of sorrow?

Can you in pure feminine wiles—not foretell that my heart is torn, ended, and

 totally broken?

Can you not dent the pain I am struck with expression of painful—broken

fingers and tattered a completely depicted soul. Have you no

compassion?

Even the sky is attired in agitation and the current and the season riled into

grieving

Chad Day

In the townland of Dromahair

Like a blank page writ as daylight

White as snow be be-bleached in Ireland

No apparent like stirs in the village at 4 a.m.

Yet the calendar reminds as the heart jumps

It Is Chad of 'Merica Day!

Chad of Litchfield

Chad of The Christ, servant to all, friend of all, scholar and poet.

So may thirty-six years prove to be constant with friendship and writing

    drawing and chant. This constant companionship of St. Chad has accompanied

me over geography and season and plain and

mountainous ridge. Brother Cedd and Patricus, Fr. Columcille and

Mother Brigid—each have influenced my path, my prayers, and my deeds.

Each of 13,141 days, each of the 315,361 hours since have hosted delight

and strengthened direction. Contemplation made whole and holy because of

    these.

Each we meet can be a blessing if we allow such to influence our outlook and

    unlooking.

Each can be a curse if we trust not and labor to much hate and not enough hope.

Child's Memory

It takes but one aslant verb or declaration

to haunt a child lifelong

One misplaced word for loathing

One for hate

One for jest

One for spice

And these are all the more memorable for their brevity

Think through the full script of a child's life

And know the memory is a precious incubator

Refine the words that shall manufacture future

To a child for it is a lasting effect and affect.

Few words about love count soundfully

Lastingly...

over the decades.

''I love you" lasts forever.

Snow Made Real

little hands proudly found the handfuls

and then formed man in his image

he is made of water that has frozen

and come down from heaven

Now at Noreaster

we have bountiful blankets of this white treasure

The stores are empty of supplies yet worry not, grocer customer come in
    droves

nevertheless hoping against hope that something may be purchased

no lories can transnavigate the iced roads

but ice is in full supply

as are friends with funny hats and smoky voices chattering away

the man of ice is coming into being.

To nature has he come to Dromahair

Now so polite toward the white drifts and covered lanes

It is perfectly clear slow and easy is the mode

walking the method

so the wind if free and may be purchased with a scarf

and joy rises up to be taken in

the snow lives for today

so we may be bold of happiness.

The Woody Tree

The woody tree

in a select Celtic forest

one may find there this species and mates

with accent and charm ever

Covered are these with Irish green verdancy

oddly majestic but mainly serine

each carries a ·secret and a signet only to be deciphered by time

This Hibernian verdancy makes for a joyful elation and exultation

happiness is being greenlike

frothy happiness fills these foresty places

time is able to ensure contentment in celebration

these are the woody trees at hunt and haunt.

Swan on a Hillside

An iterate swan most astounding

one day appears on a tall hillside

Far from any water

A lough or lake yes of course it's preferred domain

But such a graceful creature so misplaced

offends the mind

And unsettles the nerves

Startles the senses

Rattles the commonplace

How to collect one's thought after such a jolting?

How to justify the "unsuitable thing" is the question?

How to recollect one's thoughts to rights

Copasetic is far removed by a swan on a hillside

No water jostles and boggles and stunts and awakens

Surprises are ever awkward

Perhaps God uses the same to catch our attention?

Two Goblets

On a table

I set out a fair linen cloth

Ironed to perfection

Upon which I placed two crystalline glass goblets

Finely etched

Reflective, effusive of light's glimmer

these vessels held gently

a rare white wine

One for me and one for Saint Ghost

Columcille the saint of Glennveagh

Should he by happenstance

or maybe some manner

But if he come not

That is not appear

for too much work in heaven

Left to be made manifest

Then mayhaps

I myself will drink it down

and be made

Hopefully of the same happiness.

NEWTOWN

Door in Wall-Park Castle

Every door is an opportunity

it is not chance but a thousand

offerings and chances made ready

opening to salvation or the endingness of things

founding et fulfilling natures promise to thrive

so think and heavy this old wood and iron bands

lock work ancient hold the keep

the hardiness of the strength represented

suggests a bird's wing in flight at a certain angle

opening to dreams and to keeping sustaining foods in the stomach

wings work as well as are flighty

they labor as they celebrate

no wings no banquet

No strength are the front door, no safety inside?

when the hinges open "at stand," they call it

the aperture most graceful abounds

with occasion and delight

Love's "gesture bids" come in and be satisfied,

this is our finest offering, "be at peace"

an open door seems best.

Jaunty Cart et Cobb

Joseph the pull horse is a friend

He is puller of carts Jaunty

He is strength made manifest

quite the dancer he

full of cheer and humor

not much of a conversationalist

all his wits are ever about him

yet, he pauses from time to time without prompting

or permission

who knows what he thinks of?

so Joseph the puller horse gazes at life from another vantage

than we whom he pulls around pretending to see deeply

another day employed for human and puller.

WINE
COCKTAILS
A CARTE
BAR
BITES
GUINNESS
The Banker
PADDY

Dublinwinter

Cold bemoans a rattle-clack to Dublintowne

City-bustled amidst murmur unmistaken

Walkways crowded double much and bumping

Rustling youth and old shoes conjoin lingering age

Winds whip and shuttle trash upwind over the river

Birds scatter in hopes of a morsel fallen

A business of gasping and huff

Sneezing and cough

Accidental looks catch one off guard

Rigged sails once sported their sheets

Now its busses and smoke and noise

Quayside doors wink as memory passes

Time both festers and fastens

The Liffey wears its own flood of tears

Hearts have wrung themselves here before

Impenetrable skies darken towards evening

Uncommitted feet wander off in search of supper

I am here as ever passing doors and windows

Delighted for night

Now the best of evening offers tea and milk

And a warm place to sit out of the wind.

Wonder is a good companion.

Father Chardonnay

there was a young cleric from the West

who wanted to be known as best dressed

so his prayers were sublime

his oration just fine

but is better known as Fr. Chardonnay

The Pupil

Oh darkness,

Beware, guard your pride.

You boast of your fearful power and might.

Observe my creation, the eye.

The pupil is wise.

When affronted by you it dilates.

When in that state

It can find me even in my weakest amount.

I am the light of the universe.

George Sayre Jr.

Last Light

the last light of time 'o day

is the most humble of all arts

it knows if life is ebbing

the great quiet falls with the curtain of indigo and stars

perhaps some night creatures will sing and chirp some howl and wander

we humans see poorly in the darkness yet we detect the construct

but often miss the many-sided folds of grace

for grace gives rest and respite at times

and it showers kindness on worn muscles and tired feet

sore eyes may close and lull into slumber

grace as rest seems too simple to define

surely it's more than that?

the light behind the branches is subtle and slipping offstage

it shall not return for new light will be born as morning

light sublime recreated out of darkness

take in dusks painterly canvas breath the light in deeply and say thank you

and good night

in the morn new light will suggest challenges

and there will be occasion aplenty to address

new light citadel of hope

Momentary Awareness by Accident

In a hotel, maybe in Santa Fe,

A pinion fire burns in the brick chimney's arch,

Catching senses, once capitative, now freed to wander.

The soft clink of glasses in the bar simper like sweet small bells.

The haldlight calms with smoky overtones.

While the reception desk welcomes the newcomers.

The oldcomers glide silently along their own paths.

The glitz is intense but tasteful.

Elegance oozes from the floor upward.

Conversation is robust as studied verbiage.

Then the reality dawns, breaking forth, setting aside the day.

Red-orange logs topple, and a cascade of sparks showers the hardwoods.

No commotion here, just the routine of evening. All is well.

Now is the time to enjoy.

*Haldlight is a soft near but indirect illumine of a small gathering space.

Cleo's Rheel

The little people are skittish at best,

oft times e'en mannered, yet

they frolic with tankards of ale

and shamrock hats askew.

Dancing, cavorting, courtly earls and

fancy ladies laugh, and the prettiest

little one is Cleo, whose voice is angelically

sweet as she sings the rheels and notational bars

for their wit and charm, while they gather at tables

for feasting, and pots of gold provide

glimmering delight and the lilies offer

aromas allure, helping ascertain the high steps.

Also, Tythy and Lifeborn join in, most times,

to a cheer from the crowd, and all this comes by way of

well-affectioned humor, perspective,

but to the li'l ones, 'this enjoyment as central to being,

and its rule is to share the wealth.

Poor Devils All

Father Richard treads to the pulpit,

no genuflection today, bad knee.

As ever saith, he clears his prodigious frog throat,

saying, "We are all just poor devils tryin' to get through."

At thirty-four years, I detest

his summation of humankind:

Poor devils all? Really?

What does this old man-of-the-cloth know?

Then, I was at the zenith of

my intellectual snobbery or

close enough, yet now, at sixty-eight,

I humbly suggest a kinder manner,

that perhaps, as considered again more concertedly,

"We are all just poor devils tryin' to get through."

Clicking out Time

The Weatherford of London, an oversized clock, ticks

meticulous tempered agents of seconds, each prim

and tucked neatly upon themselves. Incessantly

but unhurriedly; they gather the weight of building history,

regularity controlled as best can be

maintained by mechanistic favor.

It seems earlier than usual, today at 11 a.m.,

that time is not an emotion; it is not discerned

by poetic whim but numbered accounting.

Precision is the thing of it, you see, precise and accurate.

Windowpanes in the room proclaim clarity too.

Well-kept places harness energy and open souls.

Visages of summer skip past memory as if an invitation to youth,

but as day passes, temperatures drop, holding back silly notions.

Actually, clear-freezing sunshine is its own elixir,

sincere in its strength to catch you by the breath

and set you back a footpace or two.

Yet, an invisible momentum winds the heart and turns the mind forward

as the giant clock hands etch notches of space.

Seconds of time march exaltedly but humbly, bent by the weight of life.

A Fer Fothlai (A Man of Withdrawal)

The ancient ones, Brehon at heart,

counted mercy as primmer et prime,

counseled to be additional, inclusive,

invitatory and hospitable, kind,

able to encase the Bardic preserve

of history's flash and spin, remembered

both in verse and tone, sung a steeping syllabic

tradition of clan alliteration alongside half-rhyme,

made provision for the chieftain to unite for good,

singing the songs made for unity-forged-identity

as St. Polysemous urged diversity as harmony

the many as one

and Gaelic aristocracy based upon poetry's merit

etched in Chronica's timed line, metronome exacting,

play by demonstrating skill and wit's verve to enthuse.

But, the poet must withdraw to advance societies,

Thus the sacrifus addended and turned up fine as fire

To build the libraries of annals and Hibernian decorum.

Words it is that build up, unless words rather destroy.

Let the children decide which nature seems best.

God be with them.

Adom et Eava

With mineral and humus from salt base-rock,

add water, mold, and crystal quarts laggardly,

breathing into the soggy lump

the "ruach" of living creatively;

Humanity arrives apace.

A turning point comes due; crisis dances.

The garden, ill-formed as yet, beckons.

"Make more of me that you may be more too!"

Labor on and drive incessantly into daytime.

A pond forms from morning dew

collected from the cool breezes.

Thunder roars while sun shines,

letting Creation know its Maker Spirit

is not animal-human-mineral,

but hosts far-seeing eyes, taking in

the divinity showing its angel wings outspread.

Water drips to make a lake of fantastical enormity

and clouds from overhead to rush the blood and

thrill the hearts of those blessed to be up here, up there.

Now still ye perfection, rest a moment, take-in,

Contemplate

Respirate

Cogitate

Innovate

Create as fellow artisans. Labor on.

Consider the Splendid

Like the moon's mists flying askance,

radiant cloud like morning birth alleged,

passing over with angel's wing, arched high,

Blood on lintels and limens, post and post—

The blessing from above is to pass over,

to understand the process beginning is all;

something will be lost and something gained,

all creatures destined to learn this lesson well.

And, I shall be learned only by heart undivided.

It will rise in daylight and become yesterday quickly,

the Faustus sydus, starlight in wizen eyes, no tears,

the word of prophet beaming circumfuse lux,

pouring in and around us all our days.

Today is victory appearing, bearing seen, growing bright

Firmiorem, contemplative motion, unceasing.

Assume

Assume the worst, if you must,

but gratia will be minded and won't relent.

Pure grace will overwhelm

and not dislodge the mightiest fortress.

Declare an emergency, if you must,

but reality will bear out that

there is only emergence.

Newly formed shapes, volumes, degrees

and nuances distilling the new,

willing color into annual and momentary yields

to chroma's delight and blue

Thus, even to eventual culture,

daylight truly isn't mere practicality

but more of a romance and a suggestion.

Obligation is for affection to care for the other,

the stranger, the castaways: them; they.

Walls don't embrace, nor can they contain

the divinity of spreading raw joy.

"Preparatio evangelica" is aged enough

to be sly and crafty, subterranean, if need be,

and oh, so slow going to entice, enthrall, and change.

Charge the day.

Elegiac Strophe

Ah elegy's owning power to attract

To tell, foretell the story's authenticity

To declaim out loud the meter of life

Of breath that gives hope and wish's

Invitation to 'keep at it, ' that is living

That is to find the meaning hidden

To instruct one's self in the mystery

Unfolding ever invitatory…

Ever revealing why we are here…

What does this "living" mean?

Outright," what is the purpose?"

Why existence at all verses unknowing?

"The thing of it " seems tied to fide

Fide being faith, a way of looking

A manner of seeking understanding

Like as St. Anselm offered:

Fide is seeking understanding

How you next navigate the mystery

Is up to you and if fide counts…

For some of us, it is The Measure

Of being united and at Oneness.

Herberinan Gentleness

Gentleness is passion tempered ignited then softened infused by kindness

gentleness is honed et refined as transformative offertory

a giftingness far reaching holding back nothing in reserve

this eternal affectionate giving is 'praxis' that is 'practiced'

by anticipatory awareness sensitive in-looking yet reaching forward

in refined grace as strong as iron and ancient boulders on pitch

Artistic poetries scanning in order to find a landing place for the soul

for the spirit to engage the sacred and declaim the words of 'Gratia'

Gentle down then verdant carpeted Erie

make way for the masses to come enjoy new life and dreams made sure

gentle down by invitation and hearty welcome boisterous

all the while hosting a quiet and prevenient sway and charm without end

From Irish cliffs facing westward imagine the new lands thereunto found here

all the possibilities that hope can draw and paint and intend established already

encouraged by prayers kept silent for fear of breaking the spell

gentle down then sweet Erie and its soulful yearning all who attend here

and entertain the effervescent generosity of prospective hope.

Late Spring Gale

Atlantic effusion bursting forth to the cliffs of Lion iron on West

Full throated winds hollow out crevices of net and boat rimnets remote

Gathered over winter push and strength wearing out even the ancient stones

Once bulwark but suddenly shivering in the wind tossed occasion current

This Spring which will bring its Celtic skies eventual

yet are twilighted and amber'ed as old bottles in the lough

Grayed Erie for today only; Yet will regain its verdancy tomorrow assured!

But the declination of an behindhand afternoon overwhelms with distraction

Now overtly overbearing with crowded clouds enforcing an ugly despondency

not typical to glinting sunset summer~style in western Hybernian uplands

So Tomorrow the depth and the artistry and the spited spirts will return sure

By The Celtic "Ah-yes-ness" of out-breathing sprites and joys of the little people

dancing upon heels and fiddles accompanied by ale aged to perfection in the barrels

made of dream wish fabric beknownst to all who romance fancy well.

Whistle Spirit Awakening

Whistle Spirit awakening

Sounding the life force lost in the scapes of dreamcast misted visions

hear those horse hairs on the fiddle strings tremble and quaver a sudden awakening

the old daze gone bye, or is it reality introduced once more?

Friends broken by the years dissolve and disappear in salted breezes…

A kind of poverty might ensue but not if the proper-muses kindle up the heart

Imagine they used to sing at night's break to awaken and sing your art

And as the night passed into mist and moist charity the morning's newness

abounds-kissed awake the tired faces of the village

at need of work again in sun bright illumine fully on display,

"This -This," cries out the infant in the cradle, bellows the husband in the bath

The workers in the fields bent already

the shepherd behind the sheep. Beckoning encouraging them onward

"Go now you four footed weavers" tarry not" to the glenn between

Two dramas of Colomncille who speaks still e'the morning

Unfolding the day grass dew touched and sweet. Refreshing soul and mind.

Dub brooks+ at Glenn Columncille Mmxviii A.D. +

"And here where
that sweet poet sleeps
I hear the
songs he left unsung
'At a Poet's Grave'

More Photographs

by

Dr. George Sayre Jr.

Cottage

Rock of Cashel

Thatch Roof Shed

Donegal Village

Glendalough

Glendalough

CROAGH PATRICK
IRELAND'S HOLY MOUNTAIN

Horseshoe-Shaped Garage Door

 ❧ WILLIAM BROOKS AND DR. GEORGE SAYRE JR.

Pub Peat Fireplace

The Piper's Chair

Daffodils

Paintings
by

William Brooks

Thinking Cap

Cardinal's Flight

Cleo's Madonna et El Nino

Garden dew

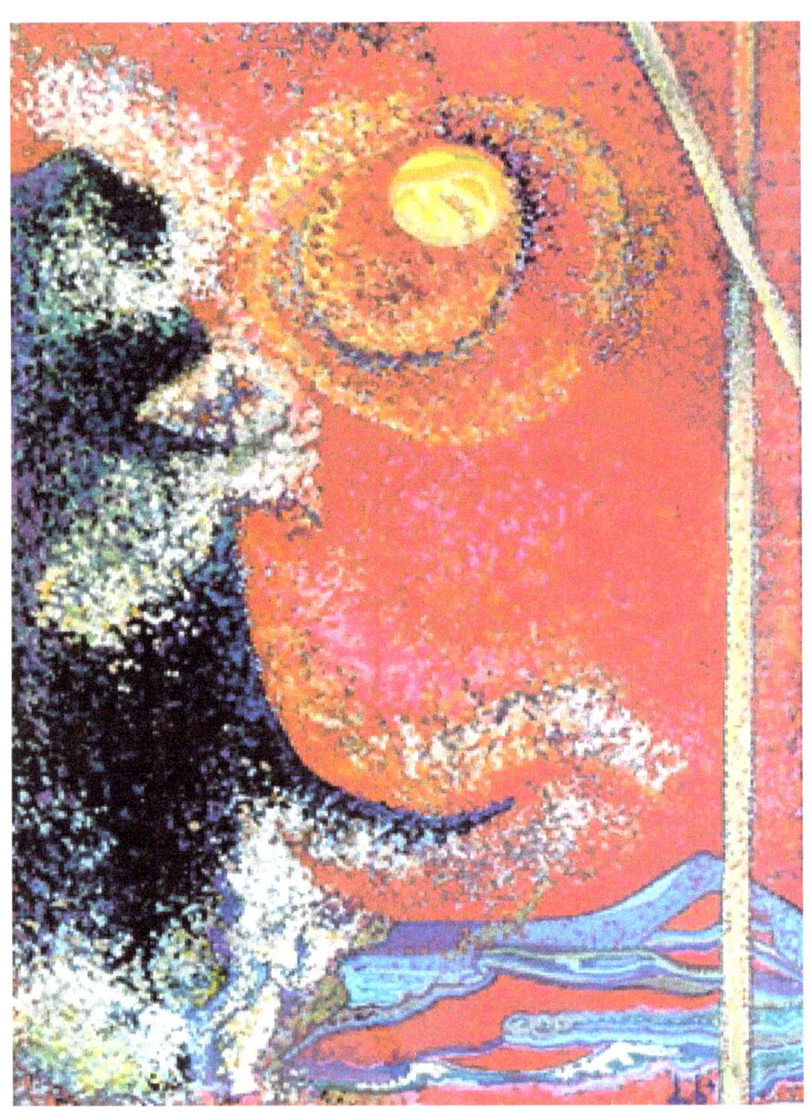

Flight 8

MidNight Garden

Heron House Shadows

June at Lake

Queen Bee

Bee Map

Molten Sun

Heather's Branches

Illumine Evincing

Illumine Evincing

Illumine Evincing

River Fox

West's Dream

Jesus Calming the Water

Angel Bride

Waterfall in Foot Hills

Easter Budding

Childhood Tree

Celtic Tortoise-Peregrinator

Hazel's Ascent

Rome at Afternoon

Angel at Burning Bush

Morning Blooming

New York Store Front

Autumnal Wind

Septembre Harvest Day

Monet's Path

Dove's Decent

Doctor Speaks to Suzanne

Night Garden Path

Painting Spider et PeaceDove

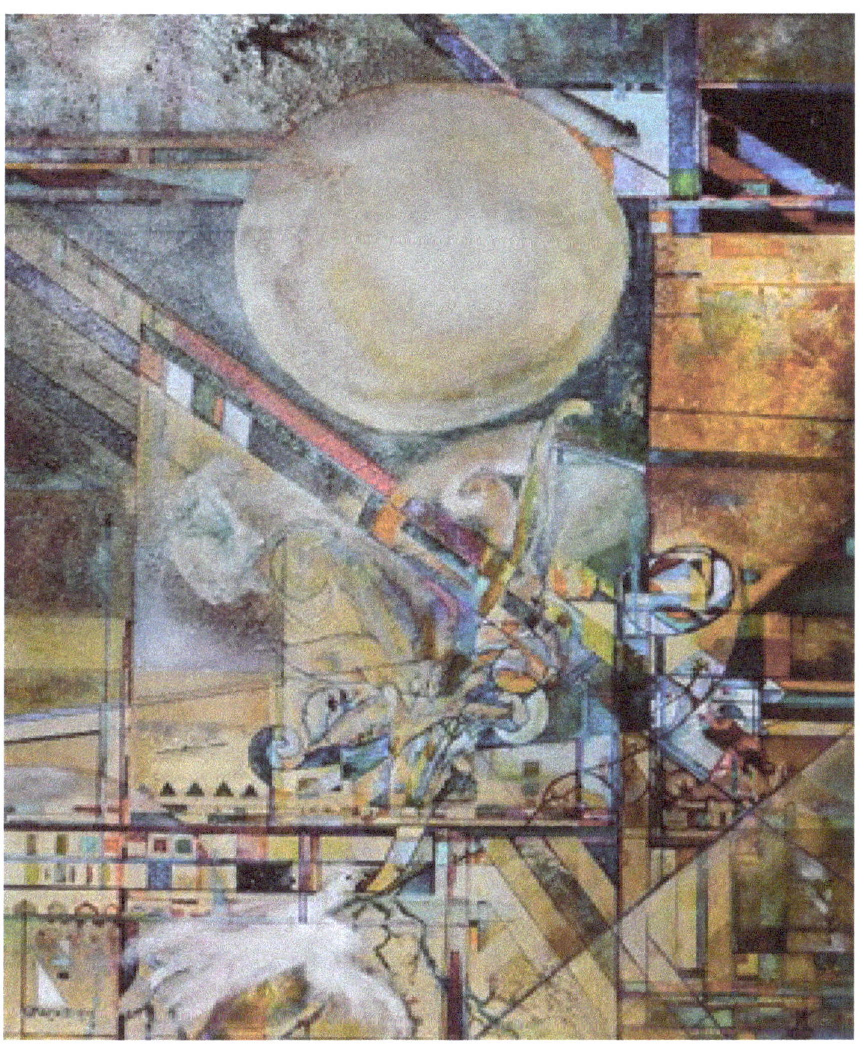

Jesus Turning Water into Wine

About William Brooks

Poet, painter, and priest William Brooks pursues the ancient past of Celtic arts and expression and modern times through the written words and spiritual deeds of W. B. Yates and St. Columcille of Ireland. Retired from three decades of active Episcopal priesthood, William now is able to study and to share even more in depth his passion and inspiration for Hybernian culture.

About Dr. George Sayre Jr.

Amateur photographer and woodworker, retired dentist and meditator, George Sayre enjoys the adventure of exploring and experiencing new venues.